H5300640

W9-BZU-209

100 YEARS OF STYLE

BY DECADE
& DESIGNER

VOLUME 2

1950–1999

This edition copyright 2001 by Chelsea House Publishers, a subsidiary
of Haights Cross Communications. Printed and bound in Dubai.

First printing

1 3 5 7 9 8 6 4 2

The Chelsea House World Wide Web address is
http://www.chelseahouse.com

Library of Congress Cataloging-in-Publication Data applied for

ISBN 0 7910 6193 0 Fashions 1950–1999 (this edition)

0 7910 6192 2 Fashions 1900–1949
0 7910 6194 9 Fashion Designers A–F
0 7910 6195 7 Fashion Designers G–M
0 7910 6196 5 Fashion Designers N–Z
0 7910 6191 4 (set)

Produced by Carlton Books
20 Mortimer Street
London W1N 7RD

Text and Design copyright © Carlton Books Limited 1999/2000

Photographs copyright © 1999 Condé Nast Publications Limited

Previous page: The 1950's shape – 'waist nipper combining corset,
bra, petticoat' – all made from the new man-made fibre, nylon.
Add graphic print and a powder puff, February 1955.

Opposite: Curve, stretch, perfect legs and a supermodel pout.
Azzedine Alaïa and Cindy Crawford – an electric combination
in his 'short and low' dress, 1987.

Overleaf: Christian Lacroix introduced the puffball skirt and 'spurred
everyone on to new heights of lively, short and seductive' at his
debut in 1987.

100 YEARS OF STYLE

BY DECADE
& DESIGNER

Linda Watson

VOLUME 2

1950–1999

Chelsea House Publishers

PHILADELPHIA

contents

1950–59

In accepting an attention from others – a drink, a light for a cigarette – it's young to look pleased, gracious and confident about it. If you hunch forward, it not only adds years, but marks you as a woman to whom such attentions may come seldom. A poised head will make you look confident even when you don't feel it.

Gestures Younger or Older, *Vogue*, November 1957

'This is the new figure,' declared *Vogue* magazine, as it defined the 1950s' body line. 'You see an unexaggerated bosom, a concave middle, a close hipline, a seemingly long leg. See it in the flesh – and in the fabric. If you weren't born with this figure, you can achieve it.' There were new ways to obtain perfect undulations: diet, exercise, massage, posture, brassiere, corset and finally, 'there is the cut of the new fashions themselves, with bulk placed one way or another'. In January 1950 *Vogue* celebrated a half-century of fashion, not realizing that it had come full circle. Instead of whalebone, there was elastication; propriety had been replaced by poise. Tiny waists and visible curves returned. The elusive beauty was back. The recent past, *Vogue* advised, should be viewed 'with amused tolerance'. Fashion was once more about illusion. *Vogue* asked, 'What is TASTE?' There were two new issues to address: class and age, as defined by dress. The rules were about to change – 'Realism in fashion designing and mass production of clothes now accent personal qualities rather than

LEFT *O Cyril our Waltz*: Antony Armstrong-Jones's dancers defy gravity. Youth revolutionized the dance floor, the wardrobe and the street, November 1959.

OPPOSITE Poise, taste and grooming were the cornerstones of 1950s' fashion. Irving Penn's portrait of elegance sums up the look, *Vogue*, January 1950.

VOGUE

CHRISTMAS
AND
NEW YEAR

OPPOSITE **'More Taste than Money'. Even inexpensive dresses were given minute attention to detail: hat, gloves, handbag and the ubiquitous necklace.**

RIGHT **Christian Dior's word was still law in the 1950s: he no longer followed a single line, but gave two opposing options – flounce or fit, 1953.**

DIOR'S BOLD SKIRT LENGTH: BULK UNDER BULK...

NEWS FROM EUROPE'S FASHION CENTRES

PARIS

...OR PARED TO A PRINCESS SHEATH

birth and wealth and have made us all sisters under the skin.' Conclusion: clothes would close up the class and age divide.

Age differences, initially acknowledged, started to dissolve. Women no longer aspired to be 30 years old. 'Young As You Are' started in March 1950 and was the first time a series of *Vogue* fashion items had been aimed specifically at the younger reader. By the mid-1950s Mrs Exeter, *Vogue*'s personification of middle-age chic, stood side by side with her teenage counterpart as she was 'invited to parties of many age groups'. Finally, age became a two-way issue in 'Clothes with no Age Tag', where *Vogue* explained: 'The fact that clothes are usually photographed on young, willow-slim models had no more or less significance than the fact that most window-displays are based on elongated plaster-of-Paris ladies with twelve-inch waists and no heads. In each case, the garment shows to its best advantage. That's all.'

The approach to beauty became other-worldly. Eyes were re-defined – wide sweeps of eyeliner flicked out at the corners, precise eyebrows were drawn – and counterpointed by dark lips and porcelain skin. Hair was brushed, coiffed and set into a sleek shape. False eyelashes were essential, mouths remained closed.

In January 1952 *Vogue* suggested additional embellishments to enhance natural coloration: 'pearls adding lustre to the skin, the kindness of dark colours, fresh carnations pinned high on a severe collar'. By the mid-1950s, mystique was dramatically heightened by the addition of a black veil over the face – 'uncompromising, it demands a degree of assurance; and as with all veiling, a master's hand with make-up'. Long, white gloves drew attention and made 'every movement of the hands a *gesture*'.

The arrival of the serene, distant beauty dovetailed precisely with the renaissance of actress Gloria Swanson. At 51 years old, and star of over 60 films, she appeared in *Sunset Boulevard* (1950), which *Vogue* described as, 'a bitter, brilliant film about a silent-screen idol who dreams of a come-back'. At the age of 43, Bette Davis made her first film in England: 'Pastel and pretty, with a tremendous personality, she once put into a film contract "in the party of the first part, I will not be required to wear any of those damned floppy hats."'

Invigorated by the new decade, designers continued their experimental line. In September 1950 Paris focused on the trumpet skirt. The following month, the watchword was 'oblique': Christian Dior's 'oblique' corselet, Edward Molyneux's 'oblique' overskirt, Jacques Fath's 'oblique' fin-flare, and Cristobal Balenciaga's 'oblique' wishbone buttoning on a wool Ottoman suit.

While Paris was enchanted with acute angles, London played safe. 'All to Match', said *Vogue*, reviewing London in September

LEFT **Hubert de Givenchy, who gave Audrey Hepburn her gamine look, trained at Fath, Piguet, Lelong and Schiaparelli. Here, it shows.**

BELOW **The 1950s' shape – 'waist nipper combining corset, bra, petticoat' – all made from the new man-made fibre, nylon. Add graphic print and a powder puff, February 1955.**

1950 and observing: 'Just as a duck demands green peas, so suits like Victor Stiebel's demand a matching velvet blouse and hat.' The juxtapositioning of complementary colour was a recurring theme, and the magazine often provided detachable handbag-sized charts to take shopping. Note *Vogue*'s 'Eye View' of the half-bought dress: 'In one-syllable words, it's not what you wear, but What you Wear with What; and this, with capital letters, is the leading theme.'

At the beginning of the 1950s it was fabric technology, not design talent, that was seen as the future of British fashion. Nylon was produced in a huge new factory in the middle of Monmouthshire, while British wool – 'acknowledged as the best in the world' – continued to be woven by craftsmen in Scotland, Yorkshire and the west of England. In April 1951, in came Chinese jackets, collarless collars, lemon yellow and mauve. Skirts that hung 13 to 15 inches from the ground, natural waistlines and black-and-white themes continued. Christian Dior was no longer God: 'Dior's collection was his best since his first sensation. Balenciaga's equalled his last year's wonder. Fath, the comet, has become a steadier star, and made a glowingly brilliant show.' These top names were joined by Pierre Balmain, Jean Patou and Madame Grès. The whys and wherefores of length were translated into question-and-answer sessions: Where is the waistline? How full is the skirt? What about sleeves? The new corsetry controlled and redistributed weight, but there was no room for manoeuvre. Dieting was fashionable. *Vogue* featured a 'Skimmed Milk Diet', 'Two-Day Diet', 'Measures for the Unwanted Pounds' and a series on 'Calorie Counting'. This coincided with Dior's 'new shaping of you'. In March 1952 *Vogue* reported the launch of Givenchy. Actress Audrey Hepburn – who later became his muse – was heralded as a combination of 'ultra fashion plate and a ballet dancer.'

In September 1952 *Vogue* noted: 'The little black dress, deceptively simple, is the core of every collection.' By the end of the year, the silhouette had curves at every turn. Sloped shoulders, cowl neckline and a small, hair concealing hat. Skirts now reached 11 inches from the ground. Designers worked from the inside out, creating corsetry to fill and suppress the seams. *Vogue* told its readers to follow their lead and 'fit the foundation to the fashion.' Dressing still required strategic thinking of the highest level: 'the sum total, a silhouette that is elegant, body-conscious, adult, becoming'. By January 1953 *Vogue*'s coverline promised 'Fashions for Flattery', featuring inside the new rounded bustline, all-in-one foundation for the moulded torso dress and nip-waisted girdle for the emphasized waist.

Fashion was a jigsaw with specific pieces: the appropriate hat, bag, belt, finishing touch. In April 1952 *Vogue*'s 'What to Wear with What' feature handled clothes in much the same way as interior designers approach decoration. Twenty-five colour schemes were put together to link in with a chart detailing colour-coordinated shoes, handbags, gloves and 'added touches' in the form of earrings, stole or belt. In the new feature, 'More Taste than Money', *Vogue* declared: 'Taste in the truest sense cannot be bought, but it can be acquired. Snobbery is the last thing you can afford.'

Photographer Irving Penn was to play a key role in creating the illusion of absolute assurance. Haughty and unsmiling, hands on hips and one foot in front of the other, Penn's visionary woman was unflustered and in control. Even so, *Vogue* lamented the disappearance of the word serenity: 'Our task is to re-establish in our minds the form and lucidity of the human drama. It is a problem of stillness, of learning how to be still, how to listen. Words are driven out of currency by our self-conscious avoidance of them.'

On 2 June 1953 Queen Elizabeth was crowned in Westminster Abbey. In September *Vogue* returned to the issues of international fashion. The latest centres were Spain, Italy and Dublin, where a new star, Sybil Connolly, presented a collection at Dunsany Castle. In Paris, Dior was again in the eye of the storm, with skirts 16 inches from the ground: 'The tumult and the shouting drowned calmer voices which might have remarked that we were wearing shorter skirts as recently as 1946.' The stalwart London designers remained united in their vision and in March 1956 *Vogue* concluded, 'London is not a city for revolutionaries: in fashion, as in everything else, she shows modernisation, painstaking detail, above all, a deep consideration for people. Here, the couturiers design for their customers, there are no stunts. But that is not to say there is no news.'

Coco Chanel reopened her salon at 31 rue Cambon, Paris, and showed her first post-war collection on 5 February 1954. She was 71. Knowing that her classic style had been relentlessly copied, she finally conceded that imitation was the sincerest form of flattery:

New assets for party faces

ABOVE **Beauty equals defined lines: on the inner eyelid, around the lips and arching over the brows, with a dusting of powder keeping it all in place, 1955.**

RIGHT **Christian Dior's 'dining out formula' of smoky lilac chiffon, wide hat, elongated gloves and the essential matching shoes, December 1956.**

'I am no longer interested in dressing a few hundred women, private clients; I shall dress thousands of women. But a widely repeated fashion, seen everywhere, cheaply produced, must start from luxury. At the top of the pinnacle – le point de depart must be luxe.'

By the mid-1950s synthetic fabrics flooded the market and stockings were 'the sheerest – 12 denier thinness, a new low (we're used to 15) just coming off the nylon machines.' A glossary of new, man-made fibres – each with its own special virtues and 'designed not as a substitute, but to play a particular role in the textile world' – included the specific properties of new mixtures of nylon, Terylene and Orlon.

In September 1956 *Vogue* reported Dior's explosive demi-longeur: 'hailed, laughed at, sighed after, feared, endlessly discussed. Is it a stunt or serious development? Should we, can we, do we want to revert to pre-emancipation femininity in the uncompromisingly emancipated era we live in?' The following April *Vogue* published its first portrait of Christian Dior, describing him as 'a man of the most admirable simplicity, undazzled by ten years of fame'. In December *Vogue* reported his death. The following March Yves Saint Laurent seized the mantle and produced the Trapeze line: 'simply the most important and fully formulated in Paris.'

Space travel was on the horizon. The Futuristic movement, spearheaded by Pierre Cardin, was already underway. In January 1959 *Vogue* described a 'Flying Start to 1959 by comet to New York': 'If you imagine a silver lamé boa constrictor with the curve of a quickly-gulped lunch inside it, this is what the Comet looks like from behind.' The gulf between America and Britain was narrowing. *Vogue*'s tone, which had echoes of the film *Brief Encounter* (1945), was being translated into teenspeak. 'Get With It', readers were told in November 1959, showing partygoers leaping in the air, captioned: '"We've so much in common, Mr Ponsonby-Ponsonby," translation: "Dig! I got the message!"' By December, the 1960s' look was defined in a seminal feature, 'The Teenage Thing'. *Vogue* relayed the opinions of a 17-year-old apprentice hairdresser, schoolboy, waitress and part-time skiffle player, dressed in the 'urban, working class' uniform of winkle-pickers, drainpipes and stilettos. 'What does fashion represent?', asked *Vogue*. 'Decoration? Armour? Disguise? A mood of society? For millions of working teenagers now, clothes like these are the biggest pastime in life: a symbol of independence, and the fraternity-mark of an age-group. Not – repeat not – the sign of a delinquent.'

OPPOSITE **Cristobal Balenciaga's melange of mixed proportions and opposing textures – taffeta dress 'with blown-up hem', velvet coat and jet bead toque, 1951.**

RIGHT **Albouy's cavalier white melusine cap, with a black flat velvet bow and a black-and-white feather like a circus pony's plume, 1954**

1960–69

I may not look like a Board of Trade official. At the risk of sounding like one I would like to say that I am not pessimistic about the future. Our assets are unrivalled. Inside this issue you will see some of Britain's amazing new achievements. Some of them are frivolous. All are wildly exciting. I am one of them.

Vogue **cover quote, Jean Shrimpton,** 15 September 1964

It took three years for the 1960s to start swinging. In 1964 slacking stopped. 'This is no place for the dilettante,' decreed *Vogue* in May of that year. 'In the general social reorganisation of these isles, one fact is clear. A new aristocracy of talent with say, the Beatles at the top and the three Etonian pop groups somewhere near the bottom – however many coronets among their players.' The 1960s instigated the catsuit, the topless swimsuit and the supermodel; with 'the Shrimp' at the beginning, Twiggy in the middle and a startling creature called Penelope Tree at the end. As the 1950s concluded, mods feuded with rockers and the teenager was eyed with fear and trepidation. *Vogue* turned a blind eye. 'Charm and an ingenue look are in tune with 1960's fashion,' said *Vogue* in January, followed by a radical re-think in September: 'Couture Clothes: are they Worth the Money?'

The 1960s turned every preconceived idea on its head. As fashion zoomed into overdrive, everything whirred in reverse. The teenager, previously *persona non grata*, had opinions and pulling power. Make-up turned from haughty to baby looks. Models played gauche, boutiques mixed genders and unisex made an entrance. Second-hand clothes,

LEFT **Vidal Sassoon's 'Rolled Florentine pageboy' haircut swept across the face, circled the brow and exposed one eye, 1969.**

OPPOSITE **Paco Rabanne – overtly unconventional – created a 'kinetic crystal gazing' kite coat, which captured the 1960s' obsession with plastic, 1966.**

LEFT Jean Shrimpton, photographed by David Bailey in 1964, in Yves Saint Laurent's schoolgirl double-breasted suit in pink lace tweed with flecks of green and blue.

But deafness was feigned. 'You go to those old buffers in Jermyn Street and tell them what's wanted, and they bow and scrape, and it's "Precisely, Sir,"' recalled a Blades' customer in 1964, 'but your suit still has twenty-five inches around the ankles and room for three of you in the seat.'

From 1960 onwards the female erogenous zone moved from demure territory – collarbone, neck and shoulder – to unexplored areas – thighs, arms and stomach. The miniskirt was one of the first fashions to filter through from the street. It was a *Zeitgeist* of mammoth proportions, worn by Mancunian art students,

once associated with charity and poverty, were chic and eclectic. Paris, veering towards a Left-Bank, existentialist look, was called, 'no dictator, but gentle persuader'.

There was a breath of fresh air in the White House, too. Jacqueline Kennedy, who had won American *Vogue*'s Prix de Paris in 1951, instinctively understood the power of clothes as political weapons. Together with designer Oleg Cassini, America's first lady formulated a quiet, meticulously groomed style, which wouldn't upset the moral majority but had youth and vitality on its side. 'She has resolutely eschewed the bun-fights and the honky-tonk of the American political scene,' commented *Vogue* in March 1961, opposite a pencil portrait of the inimitable first lady, 'and is inclined, instead, to the gentler practice of painting, conversation, literature and fashion.'

Fashion direction came from a new angle. Men, traditionally preened into submission by their partners, started dressing up. Even more startling, they had discovered colour. As early as 1961, *Vogue* noted that men had moved from regulation beige to a spectrum of brilliants. 1960s' youth was telling tailors what to do.

OPPOSITE **Flower power: Christian Dior's tall crepe trouser suit with a new clarity of line and exotic flower printing – formalized but free. Photographed in Ceylon, May 1966.**

RIGHT **By 1963 *Vogue* was featuring celebrity fashion shoots. Terence Stamp and Jean Shrimpton in 'Young Ideas High Line' – 'fresh as a baby's first dress' – photographed by Shrimpton's boyfriend, David Bailey.**

Andy Warhol
protégée Edie
Sedgewick in New
York, and pushed to
new limits by the mods. It was
picked up by Mary Quant, who marketed
the mini for the masses and produced a collection
of clothes called 'The Ginger Group'. The teenager turned into
a melange of everything pre-pubescent: *Vogue*'s 'Young Ideas' paired Jean
Shrimpton with Terence Stamp in May 1963: 'The new line is the high line,
fresh as a baby's first dress, but sharp, cool and sophisticated. Ravishing for
anyone young and slim.' In 1966 Twiggy wore a white crepe dress 'with the small
flowers of barely remembered birthday parties'. 'Young Ideas' also ran 'Skipping
Scatterbrained Summer' and, in 1966, 'It's a Small World – a two-sided story about
little girls who like to look grown-up, and big ones who don't.'

Men were turning Wildean, imitating Edwardian and Victorian eras by
wearing frills and furbelows, and allowing their hair to grow below the
collar. Reporting from Paris in March 1964, *Vogue* admitted that fashion
was looking over its shoulder. The incurable romantic was returning:
'The mood throughout is never plain pure nostalgia, never
sentimental, rather totally for the Sixties'. In London, Barbara
Hulanicki opened the first Biba store in Abingdon Road,
Kensington. It was a dimly lit celebration of Art Deco,
which also sold dreamy separates, via mail order, to
Biba wannabees in the provinces.

Couture was becoming passé and irrelevant.
Second lines – now commonly known as diffusion
– were on the increase. As London ignored the
rarefied, Paris embraced the space age.
André Courrèges, who trained at
Balenciaga, approached couture as
an engineer constructs an inter-
planetary craft. His collection
of 1965 was described in
robotic language: 'New
proportions. Click.
New fashion

OPPOSITE Foale and Tuffin combine innocence with pubescence in their 'very spare, very skimp, just a long vest' of 1965. Note the bust darts.

RIGHT Mary Quant's 'Ginger Group': the miniskirt suggested both wide-eyed innocence and radical thinking; it was always worn with baby shoes.

world. What next? Courrèges-shaped cars. Boats. Buildings. Sounds. What now? Only Courrèges-shaped girls. Like this one. If so, Go!' Hats became helmets. The skirt split in two and began to be known as culottes.

From the early 1960s *Vogue*'s fashion pages were frequented by men, chosen mainly for their intellect and humour – although sometimes a perfectly proportioned jawline would suffice. P J Proby (whose torn trousers cut short his career), Vidal Sassoon, Terence Stamp, Dudley Moore, Warren Beatty and the *Observer* drama critic, Kenneth Tynan all made the pages. Men had a fashion statement to make: Rudolf Nureyev, at 23 years old was heralded as the new Nijinsky; David Hockney, a star from the moment he accepted his Royal College diploma in a gold lamé jacket; Tom Wolfe, whose new novel, with the suitably psychedelic title *The Kandy-Kolored Tangerine-Flake Streamline Baby* (1965), gave the tailoring a literary bent and made journalism cool. Mick Jagger added sexual ambiguity to rock'n'roll: 'When he gets on stage, his striped T-shirt awry, arms, head, body moving, jigging around in an extraordinarily graceful, erotic dance, all the while shaking two phallic-looking rattles, he loses all his sweetness.'

Class barriers broke down. Pre-1960 models were aristocratic decorations with elongated family trees. Then came the beautiful quirks of fate: Jean Shrimpton, discovered by photographer David Bailey; Twiggy, a mesmerizing stick insect, discovered at 16 years old, and

weighing just six and a half stone; exotic Veruschka, often photographed with her body painted, lying in a pool of water; Penelope Tree, 'the new kind of flower child', the absolute antithesis of elusive beauty – whirlpool eyes and flower-stalk legs.

Film continued to influence mainstream fashion. There was the beret and trenchcoat worn by Faye Dunaway in the film *Bonnie and Clyde* (1967) and Mrs Peel's catsuit in *The Avengers* television programme, which sparked off legions of feline imitators. When the musical *Hair* hit Broadway, Marsha Hunt became a star, black was beautiful and whites wore Afro hair for the first time. Rudi Gernreich, California's answer to Courrèges, toyed with topless bathing suits and transparent blouses. By the end of 1964 it had become more and more difficult to shock. Encouraging innovation, *Vogue* advised: 'Look prepared for the next century'. 1966 saw the

ABOVE LEFT **The inimitable Twiggy – alias Lesley Hornby – eternally photogenic, wearing Emmanuelle Khanh's silver-studded felt culotte suit, October 1967.**

RIGHT **The photographic shoot entitled 'The Fool at Apple', which was featured in January 1968, showed the beginning of ethnic blending on the fashion pages.**

OPPOSITE, TOP RIGHT **Pierre Cardin's 'graphic new cape shape' with an asymmetrical collar and zipped at one side, worn with tight, high boots and a helmet with a vinyl mask, 1967.**

RIGHT **Strangely beautiful Penelope Tree wears a white linen outfit by Ossie Clark, accessorized with a chiffon scarf by Bernard Nevill and a Louis Vuitton suitcase.**

rise of futurist Paco Rabanne and the invention of Le Smoking jacket by Yves Saint Laurent, who told *Vogue* that he would love to find a pill that took the place of eating. In 1965 Andy Warhol, who stunned the world with his stacked Brillo soap pads and silk-screen prints of Marilyn Monroe, told *Vogue* that he was into fashion cloning and named Courrèges as his favourite designer. 'Everyone should look the same,' said Warhol, doing a perfect impersonation of an alien from outer space. They should be 'dressed in silver. Silver doesn't look like anything. It merges into everything. Costumes should be worn during the day with lots of make-up.'

Artifice increased with the space race. Before man landed on the moon, the unwritten rule, which said plastic was for picnics, metal for cutlery and paper for printing on, was thrown out of the window. Dresses were made from every conceivable material – from paper to plastic discs, leather to PVC – all cut along babydoll lines. There were obvious hairpieces and outrageous eyelashes, and hair was cut at obtuse angles, courtesy of London's most experimental coiffeurs, Leonard and Vidal Sassoon. Hairdressers, models and photographers – normally on the periphery of the industry – were the new VIPs. It was the defining moment when the world realized celebrities had less mystique, but more fascination than royalty.

In England, an art school revolution was underway, pioneered by Professor Janey Ironside at the Royal College of Art in London. The new wave of hot British talent included Ossie Clark, who graduated with first-class honours in 1965, and was photographed, hands held behind his head, wearing an op art quilted silk coat and skirt. 'I want to dress frilly people … in colours that confuse the eye,' he said. When he married textile designer Celia Birtwell in 1966 the two became twin talents, combining Birtwell's beautiful textiles and Clark's extraordinary eye for powerful sexuality. Underwear was virtually invisible. Bras – often two triangles of sheer fabric, held together by a few strips of elastic – were now so tiny they could be folded into a breast pocket. There was no visible means of support because it wasn't needed: the 1960s' chest was flat.

In the Summer of Love, 1967, Paco Rabanne's paper dresses sold at La Gaminerie on the Left Bank in Paris. Woodstock was having a hallucinogenic moment and Jimmy Hendrix said

purple was the colour of the universe. The Lord Chamberlain relinquished his powers and nudity was permitted on stage for the first time. In fashion historian James Laver's 'Instant Guide to Undress', he asked: 'Where do you go from nearly nothing?' *Vogue* presented a cultural melting pot in September 1969 entitled 'AFRODIZZYACTION', a fashion shoot which combined Clark pants, Birtwell prints, Nigerian jewellery, porcelain skin and Afro wigs by Leonard. In October 1969 *Vogue*'s 'Memo From New York' said: 'AND THE WORD IS – FANTASY. How else would we earth beings have ever gotten to the moon … October 1969, this IS the fantasy moment.' Ziggy Stardust and the Spiders from Mars were waiting around the corner.

1970–79

Style is independent of fashion. Those who have style can indeed accept or ignore fashion. For them fashion is not something to be followed, it is rather something to be set, to select from or totally reject. Style is spontaneous, inborn. It is the gloriously deliberate, unpremeditated but divine gift of the few.

Spotlight on Style, *Vogue,* 1 September 1976

Pre-empting the moment when punk clashed with the Queen's Silver Jubilee, *Vogue* used the A-word. 'You'll be wearing a positive anarchy of costume both cleverer and simpler than anything you've worn in your life,' said *Vogue* in its first directive of the 1970s. 'You are one of a kind, unique in fashion. Forget rules – you make them, you break them.' Anarchy arrived after a process of wild experimentation, the shock of glam rock, the rise of platforms, the plummeting of skirts, and the ultimate role reversal: men wearing make-up. The 1970s opened with a celebration of decoration and ended in a sinuous body line. Anarchy simmered under the surface, exploding mid-way, with a flash of perpendicular hair, safety pins and bondage trousers. By January 1970 one thing was clear: the spacesuit was not going to take off.

In the summer of 1970 the miniskirt reached the point of no return. Crotch-skimming started to look tired and out of date. 'The long skirt is here – and the first *Vogue* with not a short skirt in sight, and more leg than ever,' announced *Vogue* in its 'Eye View of A Nice Sense of Proportion' in August: 'Jean Muir's new collection says it all.' The Muir midi had

LEFT **Seventies' style: white straw hat and halterneck with electric striped chevrons above a blue ribbed waistband – Sheridan Barnett, 1972**

OPPOSITE **A mixture of the extraordinary, the Oriental and the Kabuki theatre – worn with outrageous platform boots – Kansai Yamamoto, 1971.**

Rhodes, who studied textiles at the Royal College of Art in the 1960s, started to produce her own unmistakably flamboyant clothes, which took pattern as a starting point.

The fusion between fashion and rock music, which started in the 1960s, was cemented in the 1970s. Ossie Clark was making jumpsuits for Mick Jagger. Anthony Price, who made his *Vogue* debut in October 1971 as 'an ex-RCA [Royal College of Art] revolutionary, a designer of quite some force', became responsible for styling and designing clothes for Roxy Music and dressed Gayla Mitchell for the back view of Lou Reed's 1972 album, *Transformer*. *Vogue* photographed David Bowie and Twiggy together – a shot which ended up on the cover of Bowie's *Pin Ups* album in 1973.

Orientalism was the new preoccupation. Kansai Yamamoto showed his first London collection in 1971, with *Vogue* raving

fluidity, breezed just above the calf and came to a halt 3 inches below the knee. Meanwhile, Ossie Clark staged a 'fashion happening' at Chelsea Town Hall – 'more a spring dance than a show' – with music by Steve Miller, Juicy Lucy and Hot Rats. The models wore Celia Birtwell prints, wild hair, sparkling green eye shadow and carmine lipstick.

Under the editorship of Beatrix Miller, British *Vogue* nurtured British designers, spotting and promoting talent from the Royal College of Art in London. The new breed of designer was part-textile and part-fashion designer, with the ability to switch between preparing a silk-screen and sewing revers. Bill Gibb's creations were wearable works of art, complete one-offs that were beyond a seasonal timescale. Gibb worked with a team of knitters, weavers, painters and embroiderers. 'They've added tassels and ribbons, enamelled buttons, reptile bands, Russian braid, painted, printed and embroidered patterns and pictures, made every design a collector's item,' observed *Vogue*. From 1971 onwards Zandra

VOGUE

MAY 35p

GETAWAY

Get up and go holiday fashion All-change sunshine beauty plus Vogue Living and Men in Vogue spring/summer reports

about his theatrical powers. Commercialism didn't come into it: 'Kansai Yamamoto's extraordinary evening clothes, pure theatre. Kabuki theatre. The face knitted into the playsuit and emblazoned over miles of cape.' Yoko Ono, avant-garde artist and wife of John Lennon, arrived in England in 1966 with a performance, *Cut Piece*, where she sat on stage while her clothes were deconstructed by the audience. Polly Devlin describes the chemistry in an interview for *Vogue* in 1971: 'Yoko, in antique white satin, and Art Deco shoes, plastic, exotic, beautiful. John kissed the shoe, rearranged her hair. "Why did you do that?" she said, suddenly querulous.' In February 1972 *Vogue*'s spotlight was on China. In June *Vogue* said: 'Go East! Collect flowers of Japanese culture.' The model Veruschka, who photographer Richard Avedon voted the most beautiful woman in the world, 'sits at a dressing table with her tea and honey, naked, oblivious to hairdressers, fashion editors and assistants, making up her face with a Japanese paintbrush'.

Ethnic blending was everywhere. Pablo and Delia, a curious couple who met at art school in Buenos Aires — 'looking like creatures of Bavarian fantasy, made to live in Mad Ludwig's castles' — had a vision of an exotic world inhabited by 'caricature people'. Their underground fashion statement included hand-painted, rainbow-coloured shoes and bags depicting imaginary landscapes. Thea Porter's exotic Middle Eastern upbringing translated itself into beautiful coats of brocade, silk, embroidery and crushed velvet. In October 1971 *Vogue*'s 'Eye View' presented 'The Dress you can't Date' — sugar pink, silk, wasp-waisted, with optional eras of 1937, 1938, 1948 and 1971.

Post-Woodstock, America was on a nostalgia trip. Ralph Lauren learnt his trade in retail and was one of the first fashion designers to understand the importance of sartorial storytelling, building a brand around an image. The lifestyle concept arrived. In 1973, while concentrating on menswear, Lauren designed Robert Redford's wardrobe for *The Great Gatsby* (1974). Four years later he styled Diane Keaton – playing a flaky, androgynously dressed thirtysomething – in Woody Allen's _Annie Hall_ (1977). Lauren's subsequent collections capitalized on reworking America's heritage in a modern context.

By the mid-1970s New York buzzed with a coterie of world-class designers, who were talking an international language. Calvin Klein, already anticipating the onset of the designer decade, concocted controversial advertising images with photographer Helmut Newton and built the foundations of a business that would reach an annual turnover of $500 million by 1980. Manhattan was the centre of social activity, with club Studio 54 the celebrity magnet. Halston, a great American minimalist, held court in the VIP room and had a list of socialite clients as long as his arm: Liza Minelli, Bianca Jagger and Marisa Berenson (great grand-daughter of Elsa Schiaparelli), all invariably dressed in his glamorous, understated gowns. In an interview before he hit the big time in September 1972, _Vogue_ noted: 'Halston rarely uses the word design, he prefers the word make. He insists it's the same thing.' Bianca Jagger, one of Halston's star

clients, although possessing a degree in politics, was famous for being famous – 'When she says she is the only person who has become a star without having done a thing, you tend to agree.'

In Britain, the political climate was changing. In 1975 _Vogue_ pre-empted Margaret Thatcher's rise to prime minister, showing her feminine side before she was re-packaged for the camera: 'She wears a lot of jewellery – real, but discreet. A surprisingly frivolous dress: flower-printed on black chiffon. It was cut tight in the bodice with long narrow sleeves.' _Vogue_ reflected on fashion in the past tense in its December 1975 issue: 'Seventy-five, the hinge of the decade, when we start to realise what we look like. Oh, those loon-pants and smocks! Clothes that looked best with a high wind blowing through them, free-form clothes hinting only vaguely and almost depreciatingly at the earthly reality of limbs beneath them.' Two years on, the body was taking shape, but clothes were still essentially voluminous. _Vogue_ told readers to, 'Think: Big. Think: Body Space. Learn to move inside clothes like mobile homes. Everything's made for a new race of healthy people. Do you belong?'

LEFT **Punk equalled safety pins, chains, slashes and the ultimate two-fingered salute to the Establishment. Zandra Rhodes' 1977 version was called 'Conceptual Chic'.**

Fashion's sublime paradox occurred in the spring of 1977. Britain celebrated the Queen's Silver Jubilee, punk ran riot and *Vogue* assessed the importance of royal fashion. The Firm was about to change: 'Queen Elizabeth II, her dressmakers and milliners agree, regards fashion as a duty, though one of the least tiresome of her duties. So might anyone who spends about 172 hours a year being fitted for clothes and hats.' There was also an incisive prediction by *Vogue*'s Georgina Howell: 'The Queen is probably the last British monarch who will play by the rules.'

Punk was the product of disaffected youth, whose bondage trousers, ripped T-shirts and upstanding fluorescent hair were a rude salute to conformity. The most controversial statement of the twentieth century was invented by Vivienne Westwood, a former schoolteacher from Tintwistle in Derbyshire and her partner Malcolm McClaren, who had worked with the New York Dolls and now 'mismanaged' the Sex Pistols. Together, they took London's King's Road by storm, opening a succession of shops including Sex, Let It Rock and Seditionaries. They secured their place in history by committing the ultimate act of rebellion: producing an image of the Queen with a safety pin through her nose. The sense of political unease was tangible. *Vogue* asked: 'Is this the last Labour government?'

In December *Vogue* remembered Jubilee year and in the same issue featured the Queen wearing a pink Hardy Amies silk crepe dress and Frederick Fox bell hat. 'What we do know is that she never looked better or more relaxed with colours a shade brighter, and hats more dashing.' However, this was followed by a pictorial record of punk. Propriety and subversiveness could and would exist side by side: '1977, the year hair stood on end with fluorescent dyes, the year of war paint ... Punks deliberately seek to create a style which looks cheap, scruffy and trashy. A lot of time and money may go towards creating an appearance that resembles that of a tramp who has slept in his clothes and hasn't combed his hair for years.'

1978 became the year of cults and computers. *Vogue* analysed the former, and was fascinated with the latter. 'You can have a conversation with them,' said *Vogue* in its assessment of the computer revolution, while defining the biggest growth industry as cult-spotting: 'Sociologists tell us they no longer really talk of culture among themselves but of media feedback. Many cults today have a paranoid edge to them. The Punk cult, for instance, gains its aggressive thrust from the aimless ranks of those who are young, sullen and often workless.' Punk, in its raw form, had nothing in common with regular incomes and couture salons. Zandra Rhodes took the paraphernalia – safety pins, rips, zips, spikes of fluorescent colour, eliminated the anarchy and diluted them into a collection she called 'Conceptual Chic'. 'Awful colours, aren't they?' commented Rhodes in 1978. 'When I can't decide what colours I'll have for my new collection, I try and think of what colour really grates. Now I love cheap, punky lilac. Some colours just have more of an edge to them.'

Punk made uniformity redundant. Style – an obsession that peaked in the 1980s – was the elusive quality that everyone wanted. The question was how to acquire it without looking contrived. In 1976 Vogue put the 'Spotlight on Style', pointing out that 'Style is what everybody would like to think they have but very few do. Style has nothing to do with youth ... or age ... or sex. It has nothing to do with class or colour ... or money. Though richer, as Fanny Brice once remarked, ibetter.' The indefinable was due for a makeover:

'Style is badly in need of redefinition. It's that quirk of the human psyche

which hopefully makes every millionth Chinese wear his Mao suit in a way that 999,999 had never thought of.'

The body, no longer hidden beneath the voluminous shapes of the 1970s, was fashionable – a supple body became the ultimate accessory. Vogue featured a 'superfit leotard', 'roller disco beading', 'summer's great little stretch'. In 1979 collections focused on 'The BODY in fashion': 'Hot line equals bodyline – a wide-shouldered, waisted, long-legged look.' The Lycra revolution made skintight stretch a reality and body-consciousness possible – a plus when dancing to 'Boogie Wonderland'. Vogue said: 'DISCO – the music that made audience stars – is now international, not only as a sound, but as a word and world in itself ... While the public wants to perform, disco will continue to be their stage.'

Vogue viewed 'The 70s through the Looking Glass': 'This was the decade of onion dressing. We were into crypto stripping and there were moments of peek-a-boo.' Punk – aggressive, and a complete shock to the system – was frequenting London's King's Road. In a club called The Blitz, a new style which involved piracy and pillaging, was being formed, cue: the New Romantics.

RIGHT 1970s' disco, with its flashing lights and feverish sounds, demanded a silky jersey playsuit which would allow the wearer to dance and glow at the same time.

1980–89

For the New York teenager, the European or Japanese housewife, British fashion means pop videos on MTV and splashy Di and Fergie cover stories. To the world at large, our style is that which is worn by youth as its class extremes: British fashion in international markets *is* Rock 'n' Royalty.

Rock & Royalty, *Vogue*, August 1987

Britain's new ambassador for fashion had an aristocratic lineage, endless legs, and the combined charisma of Elizabeth I and Mary Queen of Scots. At 19 years old, Lady Diana Spencer possessed a shy smile and a firm grip on the public imagination – key ingredients, which made her the most photographed woman in the world. In May 1981 *Vogue* dedicated its 'Eye View' not to the minutiae of the collections, but to the new royal arrival: 'Five foot ten and long-legged like her mother, it is rather as if a charming young giraffe had wondered into the royal enclosure.'

The decade which worshipped status symbols and courted conspicuous dressing was rooted in romantic fantasy. Royalty and soap opera lived in parallel universes. In style and content, the line between television screen and tabloid newspaper became blurred. The twin obsessions of the 1980s were *Dynasty* and Diana, both bonded by the upwardly mobile shoulder pad. By 1980 punk burnt itself out and *Vogue* entered the decade with a series of exclamation marks on its cover: 'STARS! MORE! SUCCESS! WIN!'

LEFT **The woman whose face launched a thousand looks: Lady Diana Spencer, photographed by Lord Snowdon in February 1981, before her engagement was announced.**

OPPOSITE **Big hair and a self-assured stare – only the shoulder pads are missing. Herb Ritts' seminal 1988 fashion shoot was one of the most powerful of the decade.**

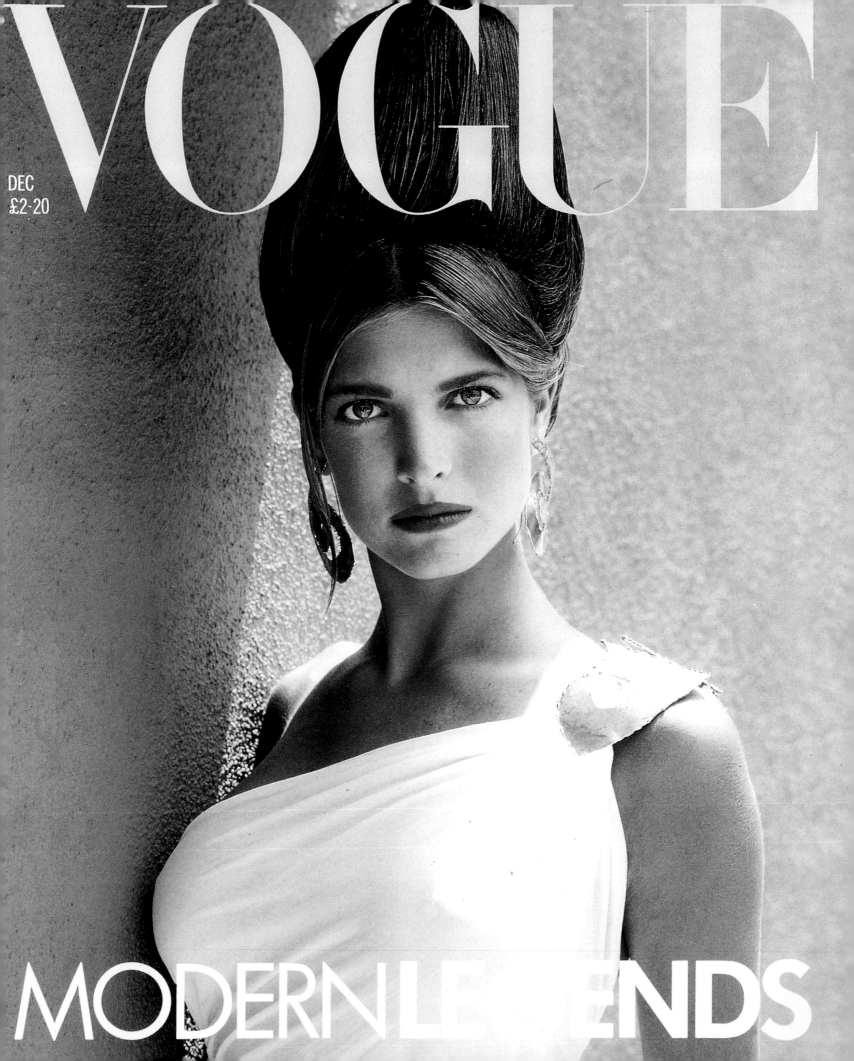

VOGUE

DEC
£2·20

MODERN LEGENDS

Vogue pre-empted the royal engagement in its 'Portrait Portfolio' by Snowdon in February 1981. It was the first official sitting of the then 19-year-old Lady Diana Spencer – 'youngest daughter of the Earl Spencer and the Hon. Mrs Peter Shand Kydd' – dressed in a cream organdie and lace dress by Gina Fratini, and also photographed in a pale pink chiffon blouse by Emanuel. In the same issue *Vogue* turned its spotlight onto America's new First Lady, Nancy Reagan: 'A character briefing, run through a computer, would read something like this: 5 foot 4 inches, articulate, intelligent, immaculately groomed … likes colour (especially red), designer fashion (especially Galanos and Adolfo).' On the Reagan way of life: 'Our style won't be the Carters' way or the Nixons' or

By 1980 Vivienne Westwood had abandoned bondage trousers and was experimenting with radical cutting. She dissected pirates, pillaged ideas from the past and opened a shop called World's End on London's King's Road, where the clock outside whirred backwards. The Japanese were already thinking along the same lines: Issey Miyake, forefather of intellectual dressing, joined by Rei Kawakubo and Yohji Yamamoto, took a more refined approach to origami pattern cutting. Japanese designers defied shopping logic by putting minute quantities of origami clothes in expansive areas of prime retail space.

Bruce Weber, who had worked on Ralph Lauren's advertising campaigns, pioneered the idea of a fashion shoot as stylish newsreel, seducing the customer with a mix of nostalgia, beauty and wide, open spaces. In January 1981 Weber was on the Santa Fe trail, shooting swimsuits in the Rio Grande, and re-creating the pioneering spirit at the TeePee Village on the Ghost Ranch Abiquiu.

OPPOSITE 'Beguia on The Bounty': Vivienne Westwood's pirate look 'in castaway cottons', which instigated New Romanticism, sold at World's End, London, 1981.

RIGHT Karl Lagerfeld arrived at Chanel in 1983 and brought with him a fresh perspective on the founder's original idea. The signature suit remained.

the Johnsons', it will be our way. We will not have barbecues, we will have music and dancing, a mixture of people and our Hollywood friends.' The royal romance coincided with the arrival of the New Romantics, or as *Vogue* called them, 'The New Elegant' in 1982: 'A fresh sartorial wind has blown across the last eighteen months. Punk dress has at last become coffee table history. Suddenly, it's cool to be glamorous.' The feature included portraits of the movers and shakers of the new club scene, including a boy called George, 'who runs The Foundry clothes shop and is a member of the band Culture Club'. In the run-up to the royal wedding, romance flourished on the fashion pages: 'Escape to the Sun. The New Romantics decked in castaway cottons, pirate smocks, pantaloons.' In June: 'Shock romance ... a midsummer night's cream, bejewelled and frilled to bits.' And July: 'There is magic and madness about – it must be midsummer. And one could hardly forget romance.' *Vogue*, August 1981,

ABOVE Calvin Klein spearheaded the American invasion of the mid-1980s, concentrating on clothes that could not be pinpointed to a particular year or season.

OPPOSITE Curve, stretch, perfect legs and a supermodel pout. Azzedine Alaïa and Cindy Crawford – an electric combination in his 'short and low' dress, 1987.

was dedicated to 'The Day of the Wedding. Official Snowdon Portraits of Princess Diana in her Emanuel wedding dress.'

Style wars broke out between the political parties. The Labour Party was out on a limb. *Vogue* took a wry look at parliamentary style: Margaret Thatcher versus Shirley Williams, co-leader of the Social Democratic Party. Thatcher: 'A slickly wrapped package. Strikingly handsome, English Rose.' Williams: 'Fresh, amiable. Looks as though her clothes were produced by a band of blind British fashion designers.'

With wall-to-wall engagements, and the world's press hanging on every seam, the Princess of Wales' wardrobe was formed. She was advised by *Vogue*'s Anna Harvey, who selected appropriate clothes and brought them into *Vogue*'s fashion room for her perusal. In her previous life, Princess Diana had worn the Sloane Ranger uniform of piecrust frilled shirt, multicoloured sweaters and Laura Ashley skirts. Now dressing turned from instinctive decision to serious business. The Princess of Wales was to be scrutinized from every angle; each minute detail – hat shape, heel height, colour,

cut – dissected and analysed. The new wardrobe was British. Among the labels were Bruce Oldfield, Victor Edelstein, Belville Sassoon and the occasional Zandra Rhodes. Diana's longstanding favourite became Catherine Walker, a quiet Frenchwoman who had made her home in London and who really understood the demands of diplomacy and discretion.

Bodymap – a design duo from Middlesex – explored radical cutting and were regarded as London's brightest sparks, bringing in the buyers and creating a stir. In Paris, Chanel had a new man at the helm. Karl Lagerfeld, who had designed for Krizia, Max Mara, Fendi and Chloé, was appointed in 1983 and picked up where Coco left off. The house had kept a low profile since her death in 1971, and Lagerfeld proceeded to take the signature to the limit, cleverly keeping Chanel's spirit but re-invigorating its classic suit through the use of new fabrics and reworked accessories, playing with new variations of gilt chains and double 'C's.

After two decades of brilliance and a quick kick of fluorescence, black became the colour of the fashion pack. In the early 1980s buyers and editors converged on Tokyo to see what was happening. When the Japanese started showing in Paris, the shade card of the chic changed to neutral conformity. Tokyo was responsible: 'What hit – and when fashions impinge in Tokyo they do so with speed and thoroughness – was very black, very big, and with a very blank look.' reported *Vogue* in 1985.

The natural antidote to frills and layering came in the shape of a diminutive Tunisian, Azzedine Alaïa. When he launched his first collection in 1981, he was quickly dubbed the 'King of Cling' and 'Titian of Tight', and given an assortment of epithets which, roughly translated, meant sexy dressing for supermodels. Alaïa adored tactile fabrics, smooth leather and substantial elasticity. Each was approached with the same principles as corsetry – holding in and pushing out. It didn't matter that his dresses were specifically built around supermodels' bodies: 'It is mystery, not nakedness, that counts. We are becoming more and more physically and mentally conditioned towards healthy living; the moulding of clothes should reflect this.' Jean Paul Gaultier, who trained with Pierre Cardin and Jean Patou, became the *enfant terrible* of the 1980s, with his conical corsetry, quirky take on tailoring and complete disrespect for conventional role-playing. In London political correctness and social awareness were the causes closest to the fashion designer's heart. Katharine Hamnett launched a 'Choose Life' T-shirt collection – clothes with a social message, including 'Stop Acid Rain', 'Preserve The Rainforests' and '58% Don't Want Pershing' (worn by Hamnett when

she met the prime minister at Downing Street in 1984). Two years later, designers banded together to form 'Fashion Aid', a benefit at the Royal Albert Hall in London.

John Galliano graduated from London's Central Saint Martins College of Art and Design in 1984 with a first-class honours degree, a collection called 'Les Incroyables', and a line-up of models whose expressions implied they were facing the guillotine. It was not until 1988 that he was on his way to becoming that rarest of breeds: a British designer with world appeal. 'To be international,' he told *Vogue*, 'is to appeal to everyone.'

Mid-way through the decade, American designers were talking concept, sensing the *Zeitgeist* and formulating collections which were flexible in more ways than one. The working wardrobe

required effective subliminal messages. The power suit, the short skirt, the heel – which said sexy but could also walk the length and breadth of the boardroom – all required a dress code that wouldn't cause alarm in the office, the bank and the stock exchange. In September 1985 Donna Karan showed her first solo collection since working as principal designer at Anne Klein. Karan's mantra was women with curves and busy lives to lead – 'clothes that would travel, interchange and impress'. Her basis was the wool jersey body suit, to which a tubular skirt, elasticated sarong or wool wrap was added, then simple pieces of 24-carat plate jewellery by Robert Lee Morris were added or subtracted: 'Everything she needs to refine or elaborate her look is contained within the collection.'

The new consumer bought Calvin Klein underwear with his signature woven into the elastic waistband. A Versace or Armani outfit could be spotted from 500 yards by the new designer literate. Gianni Versace – glitzy, glamorous and the epitome of Italian excess – presented his first collection in 1978, and by 1985 he had built, on one line alone, 70 Versace boutiques throughout the world. Giorgio Armani symbolized Milan's other side: subtle tailoring, soft shoulders, and a look that became the corporate uniform for the world's financial whiz kids. In 1987 the puffball skirt blew in and out of fashion and Christian Lacroix, a 36-year-old from Arles, France, had left Jean Patou to open his own couture house. Lacroix's lush cartwheel hats, coloured silks, froufrou skirts and seemingly irreverent approach to the reverential traditions of Parisian couture was a persuasive message for the younger customer. The following year, Diana, Princess of Wales and Sarah, Duchess of York held court to their individual sets of designers. *Vogue* cited 'Rock and Royalty: Fashion's most powerful influences' and in January 1988 switched to parliamentary matters: 'Dressing for political life is serious business; stakes are high and traps await the unwary.'

Twelve years before the dawn of the twentieth century, *Vogue* detected a disparity between designers. Some looked forward, others back; Calvin Klein, Donna Karan, Versace and Armani occupied the middle ground. Among the historians were Romeo Gigli, John Galliano and Christian Lacroix, who said, 'Every one of my dresses possesses a detail that can be connected with something historic, something from a past culture. We don't invent anything.' In the minimalist camp were Comme des Garçons, Yohji Yamamoto and Geoffrey Beene, who predicted, 'There will be a backlash against overdressing and ostentation. Economic conditions will change things, clothes will have to work for life. I don't like to look backwards – it's not fun, it's not challenging, and it's been done before.' Both designers were right. Soap opera style changed from a symphony of shoulder pads to a workable wardrobe, which appeared – even if it had an Armani label inside – to intertwine with real life. *Thirtysomething* was soothing escapism for baby-boomers, who walked around in crumpled chinos and expressed angst about their relationships. Said *Vogue*'s 'Eye View' for winter 1989: 'The first clothes we shall wear in the nineties are designed to caress the senses and soothe the spirit. The hard style of the work ethic has modulated into a new sense of the importance of balance and well-being. From eighties office clone to the nineties woman of feeling – the new psychology starts here.' Over Christmas 1989 *Vogue* reported the death of Diana Vreeland, the legendary editor of American *Vogue*, whose favourite directive was, 'astound me'. Karl Lagerfeld photographed Princess Caroline of Monaco, *Vogue* featured Diana, Princess of Wales at Highgrove with her children and picked the Mona Lisa as 'the most desirable pin-up in the world'. There was an analysis of glamour by British *Vogue*'s editor, Alexandra Shulman: 'The glamorous should not be like anyone else: Elizabeth Taylor should not have a weight problem, the royal family should not have dull, domestic spats. If glamour is a projection by the observer, whether based on envy or desire, it can always be withdrawn. Exposure and enigma are an irresistible mix.'

1990–99

Parisians do not have nightmares about being run over, rushed to hospital and caught out wearing holey grey knickers. It couldn't happen. Firstly, Parisians never leave the house in anything less than a perfect state of attire. Secondly, they do not possess holey grey knickers. Their reasoning? You wear grey knickers, your man has an affair.

French Polish, _Vogue_, May 1998

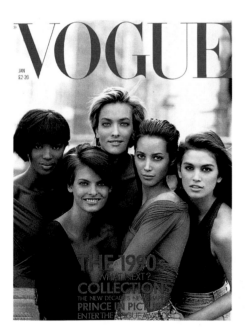

Five women who won the genetic lottery appeared on _Vogue_'s first cover of 1990. Naomi Campbell, Linda Evangelista, Tatjana Patitz, Christy Turlington and Cindy Crawford all smiled in Giorgio di Sant'Angelo stretch, faded jeans and invisible make-up. The supermodels had superseded movie-star celebrity. They were lusted after for their looks, admired for their power and revered in the 'greed is good' 1980s for refusing to get out of bed for less than $10,000 a day.

The 1990s became the decade of the mixed message. In the space of ten years, the power shoulder was exterminated, accessories escalated, the classic cardigan hit the office, big hair was cut to the quick, matt glamour disappeared, slip-dresses came out of the closet, and just when supermodels were hitting their stride, their fascination expired.

Baby-boomers had reached a point where laughter lines and middle age were staring them in the face. _Vogue_ talked about 'Real Life Fashion', with older role models arriving on cue. Isabella Rossellini signed another contract with Lancôme at the age of 39. Lauren Hutton, who had joined the Eileen Ford agency in 1966, was, by October 1991,

LEFT **The supermodel was a 1980s' phenomena, which reached its zenith in 1990 when five of its most famous faces posed for Peter Lindbergh.**

OPPOSITE **Experimental shapes for a new millennium: Givenchy, under the direction of Alexander McQueen, has introduced 'sexy structure', April 1998.**

the year of
dance
A CHRISTMAS CELEBRATION

Skirt'. What seemed an impossibility at the end of the 1980s was now set in stone: 'In Britain, the verdict is in on the long skirt. We like it.' By August the long skirt had gone global: 'Autumn 1992 is the season of the quiet revolution. By unanimous international vote, long skirts and trousers are already *faits accomplis*. The change starts with a fixed idea of elegant, elongated line from which everything else flows.'

The 1990s fashion designer no longer created clothes with complementary cosmetics and scent; customers wanted to buy into a lifestyle. Calvin Klein, whose perfumes – Obsession in 1984 and Eternity in 1987 – had captured the mood of the moment was ready to 'Escape'. Interviewed in his East Hampton retreat with his wife Kelly in November 1991, he said: 'There's going to be a big change in the nineties and it's only just beginning. The eighties were a very conservative period, sexually and in so many ways. There's a restructuring of

almost 48 years old and working with hip photographer Steven Meisel. 'One of the nicest things about Steven is the way he encouraged me to be my age,' said Hutton. 'He didn't want me to look pert, or this or that ... he wanted me to look as I felt at that time, which of course means I can feel fifteen one day and a hundred-and-fifty another – and of course look it!'

As fashion became fixated with the here and now, there were two major fashion flashbacks. Just as the 1970s had resurrected the 1920s and 1930s, so the 1990s reinvigorated the 1960s and 1970s with flares (later called bootlegs) and platform shoes. In spring 1990 stretch leggings replaced tailored trousers, with Pucci print versions the must-have of the moment.

By 1992 the power suit had been given the last rites and in July of that year *Vogue* sounded the death knell when it said, 'RIP The Short

ABOVE **Diana, Princess of Wales was** ***Vogue*'s cover girl in December 1991 for the first time since her marriage – wearing a black polo neck, with a new tousled haircut.**

RIGHT **The Versace dress from the spring/summer 1994 collection, which made actress Elizabeth Hurley's career and put a new slant on safety pins.**

priorities. It's less about flash and more about people in the streets, the environment. People are becoming more real.' In September 1994 Ralph Lauren, photographed at his 250-acre estate in Bedford, New York, became past master of retail seduction: 'I like faded and old, you know, I *like* shabby. It's not a mania for Englishness, it's a matter of ... integrity.'

British *Vogue* celebrated its seventy-fifth anniversary in June 1991, with Linda Evangelista, Christy Turlington and Cindy Crawford on the front cover. In December the cover girl was Diana, Princess of Wales, photographed by Patrick Demarchelier and sporting a new, short haircut, courtesy of Sam McKnight. She wore a plain black sweater, her chin resting on her hands. The royal divorce meant that the former HRH was free to dress as she pleased. Protocol no longer mattered. Valentino, Chanel, Lacroix and Versace were all sported as the newly single princess started to show the hallmarks of someone starting afresh: lower necklines, shorter skirts and – now that she was no longer concerned about towering over her husband – higher heels.

London was on the brink of a fashion renaissance not seen since the 1960s. Alexander McQueen graduated from Central Saint Martins College of Art and Design in 1992 and his work appeared for the first time in British *Vogue* in November of that year, worn by *Vogue* stylist Isabella Blow. McQueen's opening gambit – bumster trousers – divided the press. Although fans said they were the best thing since sliced bread, the critics pointed out that bumsters – low-slung trousers which left little to the imagination – were par for the course on building sites. The following year, grunge – a sub-culture which started in Seattle, USA – spawned a new kind of fashion shoot and a different way of posing. Kate Moss captured the look in *Vogue*'s first grunge shoot in 1993, photographed in a sparse flat with a suitably vacant expression.

When Elizabeth Hurley arrived at the premiere of the film *Four Weddings and a Funeral* (1994), her curves held in place by Versace's silk crepe and a series of safety pins, notoriety and a lucrative Estée Lauder contract followed. In 1998 the memory had transcended into fashion history: 'Her arrival in "that" Versace dress has the same kind of significance in tabloid folklore that the Nativity does to Christians: the moment at which a star was born.' *Vogue*'s Christmas 1993 issue featured two new models and paved the way for the modern aristocratic muse: Honor Fraser,

RIGHT Kate Moss, complete with fairy lights, wore a Liza Bruce vest and translucent G-string to star in *Vogue*'s first grunge shoot, June 1993.

photographed at the family seat in Inverness-shire, and Stella Tennant, in a dilapidated part of Spitalfields, east London, sporting a ring through her nose. However, Cindy Crawford faced a far more pressing dilemma than which designer to wear: she was getting older. With a fashion consensus that was saying young, gauche and skinny, Cindy Crawford was curvy, womanly and nudging 30. 'She recently turned down the idea for a Cindy Doll, complete with mole, which would have made her a ton of money,' reported *Vogue*. 'I'd get too much shit for doing that. In my mind, I kept seeing the promotional picture of me holding a doll dressed in exactly the same clothes I was wearing. That picture would speak a thousand words – and they're not the thousand words I want spoken.'

In 1990 Marc Bohan, ex-Dior designer, was asked to take over at Norman Hartnell in London. Then, in November 1995, John Galliano made history as the first British designer to be appointed

head of a French couture house when he went to Givenchy. Two years later he was head-hunted by Dior and presented his first collection in January 1997. It was a pivotal moment for Paris couture and the fulfilment of a delicious dream for Galliano. When Gianfranco Ferre left a vacant space at Christian Dior, musical chairs commenced: Galliano went to Dior, Alexander McQueen went to Givenchy and Stella McCartney took over at Chloé. Then the Americans landed: Michael Kors was appointed at Céline and Narciso Rodriguez – a virtual unknown until he designed Carolyn Bessette Kennedy's wedding dress in 1996 – took over the helm at Loewe. Marc Jacobs moved to Louis Vuitton and Alber Elbaz, a protégé of Geoffrey Beene, went to Guy Laroche and later to Yves Saint Laurent, overseeing the ready-to-wear collection while the maestro concentrated on couture.

Just as the four fashion capitals achieved equal footing, they were joined by a fifth: in Belgium, Dries Van Noten, Martin Margiela and Ann Demeulemeester comprised a new brand of fashion intelligentsia, which was on a par with the Japanese. *Vogue* took a wry look at the breed: 'While still at kindergarten in Antwerp, the Belgian designer had a strong vocational calling. But ten years and three Patti Smith albums later, she discovered that you don't have to be a Carmelite nun to wear groovy black clothes. Designers, too, can credibly go the Goth route.'

Designer logos no longer shouted conspicuous consumption, but whispered subliminal messages. The Gucci snaffle, the Hermès bag, the small but perfectly formed Prada triangle in silver and black were all 1990s' symbols for chic and hip, understood only by those who knew the precise code. Martin Margiela headed Hermès; Tom Ford gave Gucci a new lease of life. Even though the designers were high profile, it was the brand and not the individual that was gaining momentum.

As the millennium drew closer, *Vogue* traced the disappearance of the Chanel button and the death of the personal trainer. The 'in' accessory was a more accessible way of giving potential customers a piece of the action. During the 1990s, style switched seasonally, from Prada's nylon bag to Fendi's baguette. Eventually, the designer bag wasn't held in the hand but, instead, hugged the body. London produced designers who were being taken very seriously. Hussein Chalayan, who veered more towards fine art than fashion, was one of the few British designers to focus on minimalism, designing cashmere for TSE in New York and dressing Icelandic singer-songwriter Björk: 'Fashion is so transient now. I'm trying to give my work constant development – both conceptually and aesthetically. Sex has always sold fashion, and I'm just tired of it.' The sudden, tragic death of Diana, Princess of Wales was marked with a tribute by *Vogue*'s Anna Harvey in October 1997: 'It is said she was more beautiful in the flesh. Once, on a visit to *Vogue*, the art department, who'd been quite cynical about her, were agog. She had sparkle. It was simply magnetic and, in the end, it transcended her clothes.'

OPPOSITE British designer and 'earnest philosopher', Hussein Chalayan, experimented with paper and tailoring in this Gold Tyvek floral-printed suit.

BELOW John Galliano at Christian Dior in 1997, doing what he does best: taking a slice of history – corsets and patterned silks – and injecting modernism.

LEFT 'Skin on Skin': Ann
Demeulemeester's leather
halterneck worn by Stella
Tennant, the new breed of
aristocratic British model.

OPPOSITE Prada's latex strip
skirt, wool Lurex top and leather
boots by Manolo Blahnik were
photographed by Nick Knight
for *Vogue*'s 'Light Future', 1999.

The fashion show became a new form of performance art. Alexander McQueen was becoming just as famous for theatrics as his avant-garde attitude to cutting. 'Alexander said he wanted the paint guns to look like snakes rearing up to attack,' *Vogue* reported of his show that simulated urban carnage with burning cars. 'When people started rioting to get in, I remember running backstage and thinking, "Well, Alexander's famous now."'

Author Helen Fielding, alias Bridget Jones, scored a double whammy when she tapped into one of the most important social changes of the century and added 'singleton' and 'smug marrieds' into the general vocabulary. 'The office for National Statistics predicts that by the Year 2000, a quarter of all women will be single.' For the woman with an escalating disposable income and a tenuous grasp on her emotions, retail therapy was a soother of senses; a tangible form of spiritual uplift, a new kind of designer deliverance.

At the first couture collection after her brother Gianni's death in 1997, Donatella talked about diluting full-on Versace glamour and concentrating on more refined designs: 'That's what people really wear. I want to make clothes that can be worn all the time but are still extraordinary.' Women began searching for something more meaningful than designer labels and desirable logos: antique clothes with a sense of history. *Vogue* wrote, 'As we head towards 2000, fashion is travelling back in time to the *fin de siècle*, when femininity held sway and the emphasis was on soft sensuality.' In 1999 *Vogue* focused on 'Fashion's New Medicis' – designers who were moving into the art world. When Gucci sponsored 'The Work of Charles and Ray Eames' at London's Design Museum in 1998–1999, the museum's director said: 'Let's face it, more people have heard of Gucci than the Eameses.' Discussing his collaboration with artist Jenny Holzer, Helmut Lang told *Vogue* he wanted to develop a perfume that 'would smell of the human body – like clothes that had been worn but were still fresh'.

RIGHT Eclectic antique clothing,
or collections which gave that
sensation, ran parallel to purism
at Dries Van Noten's autumn/
winter 1998 collection.

INDEX

PICTURE CREDITS

The publishers would like to thank the following sources for their kind permission to reproduce the pictures in this book:

t: top, b: bottom, l: left, r: right, tl: top left, tr: top right, bl: bottom left, br: bottom right, bc: bottom centre, bcl: bottom centre left, bcr: bottom centre right.

All images © Vogue, The Condé Nast Publications Ltd./
Tony Armstrong-Jones 6
Clive Arrowsmith 23
David Bailey 15, 17tl, br, 21, 24b
Eric Boman 27
Rene Bouche 9tr, 11t
Alex Chatelain 32, 34
Henry Clarke 9bl, 12, 13, 16
Corinne Day 41
John Deakin 8
Patrick Demarchelier, 3, 4, 33b, 35, 36, 40t
Anthony Denney 1, 10
Terence Donovan Archive 42
Arthur Elgort 22, 33t, 43
Hans Feurer 14
Oberto Gili 39
Hulton Deutsch Collection/Corbis (jacket)
Just Jaeckin 19
Andrew Lamb 29, 40b, 44b
Barry Lategan 24t, 26
Roger Law 18
Peter Lindbergh 37, 38
Frances McLaughlin-Gill 11b
Tom Munro 45
Irving Penn 7
Herb Ritts 31
Robert 25
Lothar Schmid 28
David Sims 44t
Lord Snowdon 30
Ronald Traeger 20tl, tr, b

Every effort has been made to acknowledge correctly and contact the source and/copyright holder of each picture, and Carlton Books Limited apologizes for any unintentional errors or omissions which will be corrected in future editions of this book.

ACKNOWLEDGEMENTS

Very special thanks to Erika Frei for her encouragement and advice on the fine art of tact and diplomacy. To Joyce Douglas for being there.

Thank you to Vogue's superb library staff – Darlene Maxwell, Chris Pipe, Nancy Kim, headed by the brilliant Lisa Hodgkins – for their support, good humour and company throughout this project.

Two people who were fundamental: endless thanks to Francesca Harrison, picture editor, for being calm, efficient and having a lovely eye. Emily Wheeler-Bennett, Condé Nast's editorial business and rights director, for being a complete professional and friend.

This book is dedicated to my mother, father and brother Billy with love.